Hustling and Bustling
PLANES

WHEELS AND
AUTOMOBILES

FOX EYE
PUBLISHING

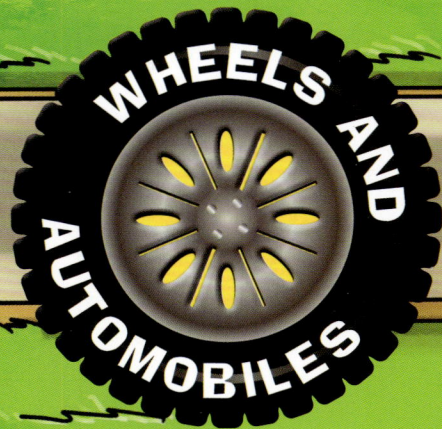

A plane is a machine that helps us travel far and wide.

All around the world, planes whizz across the sky.

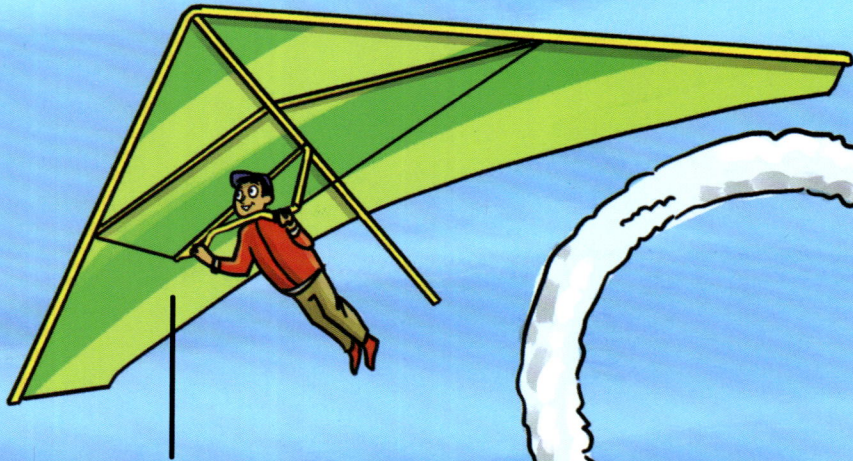

hang glider

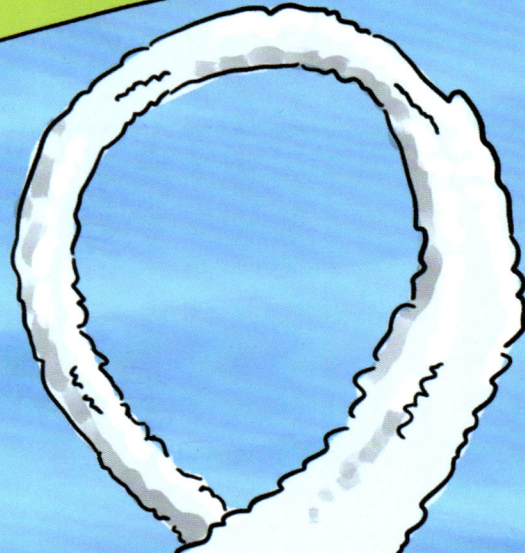

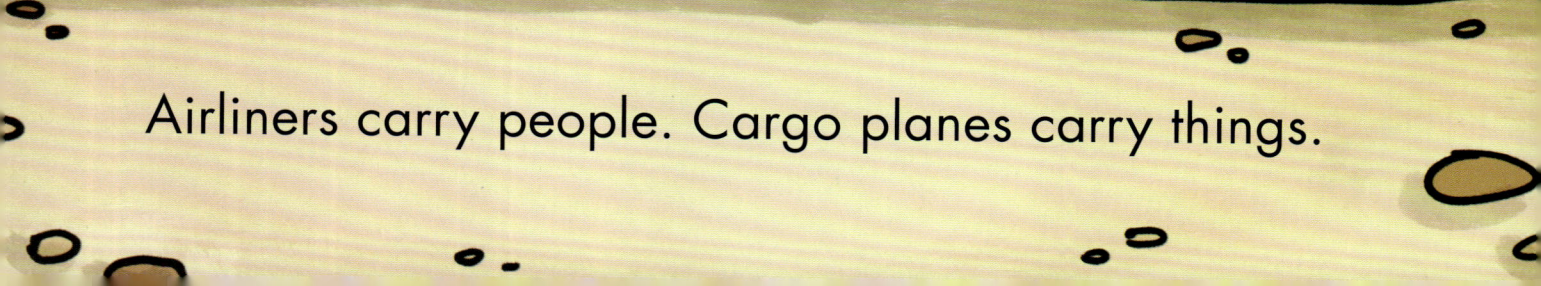

Airliners carry people. Cargo planes carry things.

Some planes do tricks and, just for fun,
hang gliders move with silent wings.

Some planes are small. Some planes are large.
Some land upon the sea.

Some land upon the ground. How many can you see?

This seaplane floats on water and takes off from the sea.

float

It has a large float on each side, instead of landing wheels.

Over Buckingham Palace the Red Arrows fly,

painting red, white and blue lines in the sky.

pilot

The pilot is in the cockpit.
The plane is ready to take to the skies.

passengers

The passengers all climb aboard.
They are going for a fly!

The pilot starts the engine. It makes a roaring sound.

wheels

The engine makes the plane move.
The wheels turn round and round.

runway

The plane rolls down the runway.
It is moving very fast.

wings

The wind moves beneath the wings.
It lifts the plane at last.

Inside the plane the passengers sit in rows of seats.

The cabin crew are handing out
things to drink and eat.

The plane soars up above the clouds. The houses look tiny below. The plane soars over mountains and seas. Now where will it go?

The rudder turns the plane around. The pilot brings it down low. The plane lands back on the ground – home again, safe and sound!

Bustling Words

Airliners are planes that carry only people.

Cargo planes are planes that carry only goods, which are things that people need or want.

A **cockpit** is part of a plane in which a pilot sits.

An **engine** is the part of a plane that makes its energy.

Hang gliders are used for fun. People hold on to hang gliders and jump off high places. They then glide, or fly easily, on the wind.

A **machine** is something that helps us to do work.

Passengers are people who travel on a plane.

A **rudder** is part of a plane that helps to turn it left or right.

A **runway** is a long strip of land on which a plane travels to take off, or lift up into the air, or land.

Soars means to fly easily in the air.

Travel means to move from one place to another.

Wings are parts of a plane that stick out from its sides. They help lift the plane up in the sky.

First published in 2024 by Fox Eye Publishing
Unit 31, Vulcan House Business Centre,
Vulcan Road, Leicester, LE5 3EF
www.foxeyepublishing.com

Author: Katherine Eason
Art director: Paul Phillips
Cover designer: Emma Bailey
Editor: Jenny Rush

All illustrations by Eszter Szepvolgyi

978-1-80445-337-7

Printed in China